American English Slang:

Dialogues, Phrases, Words &

Expressions for English Learners

Jackie Bolen

www.eslspeaking.org

Table of Contents

About the Author: Jackie Bolen

I taught English in South Korea for 10 years to every level and type of student. I've taught every age from kindergarten kids to adults. Most of my time has centered around teaching at two universities: five years at a science and engineering school in Cheonan, and four years at a major university in Busan where I taught upper level classes for students majoring in English. In my spare time, you can usually find me outside surfing, biking, hiking, or snowshoeing. I now live in Vancouver, Canada.

In case you were wondering what my academic qualifications are, I hold a Master of Arts in Psychology. During my time in Korea I successfully completed both the Cambridge CELTA and DELTA certification programs. With the combination of almost ten years teaching ESL/EFL learners of all ages and levels, and the more formal teaching qualifications I've obtained, I have a solid foundation on which to offer advice to English learners.

I truly hope that you find this book useful. I would love it if you sent me an email with any questions or feedback that you might have.

Jackie Bolen (www.jackiebolen.com)

Twitter: @bolen_jackie

Email: jb.business.online@gmail.com

You may also want to check out these other books by Jackie Bolen. It's easy to find them wherever you like to buy books.

- English Collocations in Dialogue

- Advanced English Conversation Dialogues

- 1001 English Expressions and Phrases

Introduction to American English Slang

Welcome to this book designed to help you expand your knowledge of slang in American English. My goal is to help you speak and write more fluently.

Let's face it, English can be difficult to master, even for the best students. In this book, you'll find dialogues that are ideal for intermediate-level students.

The best way to learn new vocabulary is in context.

To get the most bang for your buck, be sure to do the following:

– Review frequently.

– Try to use some of the phrases and expressions in real life.

– Don't be nervous about making mistakes. That's how you'll get better at English!

– Consider studying with a friend so you can help each other stay motivated.

– Use a notebook and write down new words, idioms, expressions, etc. that you run across. Review frequently so that they stay fresh in your mind.

– Be sure to answer the questions at the end of each dialogue. I recommend trying to do this from memory. No peeking!

– I recommend doing one dialogue a day. This will be more beneficial than finishing the entire book in a week or two.

Good luck and I wish you well on your journey to becoming more proficient with American English slang.

Chill Out

Keith is telling Sam that he's going to leave.

Keith: Hey, I think I'm going to **bail**.

Sam: **Chill out**! You just got here. Why are you leaving?

Keith: I'm tired of playing **third wheel** with you **couch potatoes**.

Sam: Come on stay. We'll watch **a flick** or something.

Keith: Nah, I'm going to **roll**. I want to **catch some rays** at the beach.

Sam: You're such **a pain in the neck**! Why don't we come with you though? I'm tired of sitting around too.

Vocabulary

Bail: Leave; depart.

Chill out: Relax.

Third wheel: Describes someone who is spending time with a couple.

Couch potatoes: People who aren't that active, instead preferring to sit on the couch and watch TV or play video games.

A flick: A movie.

Roll: Go somewhere.

Catch some rays: Go outside in the sun.

A pain in the neck: Describes someone who is annoying or bothersome.

Practice

Fill in the blanks with the correct word or phrase.

1. My youngest is such _____.

2. Let's _____. There are some weird people here.

3. I don't mind being the _____, depending on the couple.

4. Let's _____. We need to be there in 15 minutes.

5. I want to _____ this weekend for sure.

6. Hey, _____. We don't have to be there for another hour.

7. Do you want to catch _____ this weekend?

8. My kids are basically _____ and never want to go outside.

Answers

1. a pain in the neck

2. bail

3. third wheel

4. roll

5. catch some rays

6. chill out

7. a flick

8. couch potatoes

My Bad

Owen is apologizing for cancelling a plan with Nate.

Nate: Hey, so what happened last night? We were supposed to **hang out.**

Owen: My bad. I **pulled an all-nighter** the night before and **crashed** hard. I didn't even see your messages until this morning.

Nate: Okay. **No worries**. It was a **bummer** though! I wanted to see you. I did **hit the books** though for that test next week so **not all was lost**.

Owen: Are you free this weekend? Let me buy you dinner to make up for it.

Nate: **I'm down**. Friday night?

Owen: Perfect.

Vocabulary

Hang out: Spend time with someone.

Pulled an all-nighter: Stayed up the entire night to study or work.

Crashed: Suddenly had no energy.

No worries: It's okay.

Bummer: Too bad.

Hit the books: Studied.

Not all was lost: There was something positive in a bad situation.

I'm down: An expression that shows you want to do the thing that the other person is suggesting. Same as, "I'm in."

Practice

Fill in the blanks with the correct word or phrase.

1. _____ with whatever. What are you thinking?
2. Oh, _____. I don't even care about that.
3. I _____ last week and I'm still tired from it.
4. Bobby, you need to _____. Isn't your test tomorrow?
5. Do you want to _____ this weekend?
6. It was annoying but _____. We were able to recover the data.
7. I _____ so hard last night after 10 hours at the beach.
8. That's a _____ about your car not starting.

Answers

1. I'm down
2. no worries
3. pulled an all-nighter
4. hit the books
5. hang out
6. not all was lost
7. crashed
8. bummer

Pit Stop

Ted and Ryan are on a road trip.

Ted: Hey buddy, can we make a **pit stop**? I need to **drain the lizard**.

Ryan: **Gross**. **TMI**. Can you make it to a gas station without having a **meltdown**?

Ted: Ummm...maybe not. Just **pull over**, okay? Or you might have to do **damage control**.

Ryan: Okay! Hurry up though. I'm getting **hangry** and want to get something to eat.

Ted: Okay. I will! I know how grumpy you get when you don't eat breakfast.

Vocabulary

Pit stop: Stopping to get snacks or go to the bathroom on a road trip.

Drain the lizard: Go to the bathroom.

Gross: Disgusting.

TMI: Too much information. Used to express displeasure when someone tells you something that you think should be kept private.

Meltdown: Temper tantrum.

Pull over: Stop the car on the side of the road.

Damage control: Trying to contain a bad situation.

Hangry: Hungry + angry combined

Practice

Fill in the blanks with the correct word or phrase.

1. I always get so _____ when I skip breakfast.
2. I need to _____ before we leave.
3. My son had a huge _____ this morning about what to wear to school.
4. We'll need to do _____ on this one. The report has already leaked out.
5. Stop right there! It's already _____.
6. Can we make a _____, please? I'd love to get another coffee.
7. Please _____ right now. I'm feeling carsick.
8. So _____. Did you see that guy pick his nose?

Answers

1. hangry
2. drain the lizard
3. meltdown
4. damage control
5. TMI
6. pit stop
7. pull over
8. gross

Dumped

Alex got dumped by his girlfriend.

John: Hey **bro**, what's up? You don't look so good.

Alex: I just got **dumped** by Kendra. And just when we started talking about **getting hitched.**

John: Sorry to hear that. Wasn't she super **flakey** though, always cancelling at the last minute?

Alex: Yeah, and I **straight up** caught her lying to me more than a few times.

John: Better off without her. Let's get **ripped** this weekend. It'll take your mind off of it.

Alex: Yeah, I want to **blow off some steam**. Just don't post about it on social media. I don't want to get **busted** by my boss. He just **added me** as a friend on Facebook.

Vocabulary

Bro: A way to greet a close male friend (if you're also a guy).

Dumped: Broken up with.

Getting hitched: Getting married.

Flakey: Describes someone who doesn't follow through with what they say or always cancels plans.

Straight up: Speaking honestly.

Ripped: Drunk.

Blow off some steam: Relax; let loose.

Added me: Becoming friends with someone on social media.

Practice

Fill in the blanks with the correct word or phrase.

1. What do you like to do to _____?
2. I'll never work on another project with her if I can avoid it. She's so _____.
3. I got _____ last night at the work Christmas party. I hope that I didn't do anything too embarrassing.
4. Did you hear that Ted _____ Lindsay?
5. My grandma just _____ on Instagram. It's so cute!
6. I _____ never want to talk to that guy again.
7. Tom and I are _____ next month.
8. Hey _____, how are you doing these days?

Answers

1. blow off some steam
2. flakey
3. ripped
4. dumped
5. added me
6. straight up
7. getting hitched
8. bro

Hooked On

Kerry and Sabrina are talking about snowboarding.

Kerry: Hey Sabrina, you're looking good these days! What's up?

Sabrina: I'm **hooked** on snowboarding. I have a few **epic fails** but no broken bones yet. I've been going every weekend.

Kerry: **Sick**! Where do you go?

Sabrina: Whistler usually. I have a season's pass.

Kerry: Did you pick up some **wheels**? How do you get there?

Sabrina: Yeah, I just bought a used car!

Kerry: **Sweet**. That sounds awesome.

Sabrina: Do you board? We can go together.

Kerry: **I'm game**. I haven't gone in years but it's **a piece of cake**, right?

Sabrina: Yeah, it's just **like riding a bike**. Seriously, let's go next weekend.

Vocabulary

Hooked: Addicted.

Epic fails: Major problems.

Sick: Awesome; great.

Wheels: A car.

Sweet: Great!

I'm game: I want to do it.

A piece of cake: Describes something that's easy to do.

Like riding a bike: Describes something that you can easily do after many years of not doing it.

Practice

Fill in the blanks with the correct word or phrase.

1. Don't worry about that test. I wrote it last year and it was _____.
2. _____! I loved that new video you just posted.
3. You'll be fine. It's just _____.
4. _____ for whatever. Just let me know the plan.
5. I'm so _____ on The Queen's Gambit.
6. Once you get some _____, you'll never want to go back to taking the bus.
7. That's a _____ bike you have there.
8. We had a few _____ at the beginning of the project but things are running smoothly now.

Answers

1. a piece of cake
2. sick
3. like riding a bike
4. I'm game
5. hooked
6. wheels
7. sweet
8. epic fails

The Chicken or the Egg

Bob and Sam are talking about Sam's son.

Bob: Hey, how's your son doing these days? I heard he got into a bit of trouble?

Sam: He **drives me up the wall**. He's both a **slacker** and a **stoner.** I don't know if it's **the chicken or the egg** but whatever the case, he's **flunking** out of high school because he's always **high**.

Bob: You were such a **keener** in school. How did this happen?

Sam: Trust me. I have no idea.

Bob: What does he say when you talk to him?

Sam: He just yells, "**Get off my back**!" We can't even have a real conversation about it. I'm scared he's ruining his life.

Bob: Well, I'm here for you if you need to talk about things.

Vocabulary

Drives me up the wall: Makes me crazy.

Slacker: Describes someone who is lazy.

Stoner: Describes someone who likes to do illegal drugs often.

The chicken or the egg: Which thing comes first?

Flunking: Failing.

High: On drugs.

Keener: Describes someone who is the opposite of lazy.

Get off my back: Stop bugging me.

16

Practice

Fill in the blanks with the correct word or phrase.

1. Seriously, _____. I don't want to talk about this anymore.
2. It _____ when he doesn't put his dishes in the dishwasher.
3. You're such a _____, studying two weeks before the test.
4. Is it _____? It's difficult to tell in this situation.
5. Let's get _____ after work tonight.
6. I was a _____ in high school but I quit when I went to university.
7. I'm _____ math but I don't care.
8. My daughter is a _____ and doesn't care about school. She'd rather just hang around with her friends.

Answers

1. get off my back
2. drives me up the wall
3. keener
4. the chicken or the egg
5. high
6. stoner
7. flunking
8. slacker

Rinky-Dink

Mary, Sam, and Annie are friends who are at their high school dance.

Mary: Hey **ya'll**. Let's **split**. This dance is so **rinky-dink**.

Annie: Yeah for real. **Corny** is the only word for it.

Sam: Do you want to head back to my **pad**? We can **nuke** some pizza pockets and watch a movie or something?

Mary: I'm **bummed** about leaving. I had such **high hopes**. But yeah, I'm in. Let's go.

Annie: I'll come too. Should we ask Tony?

Sam: Nah, let's keep it small. My parents will get **pissed** if too many people come over.

Vocabulary

Ya'll: A way of addressing more than one person, commonly used in the Southern USA.

Split: Leave.

Rinky-dink: Small or amateur.

Corny: Cheezy, not slick.

Pad: Where someone lives; place of residence.

Nuke: Microwave (verb).

Bummed: Feeling let down about something.

High hopes: High expectations.

Pissed: Angry.

Practice

Fill in the blanks with the correct word or phrase.

1. I had _____ for that movie. Why did everyone think it was so good?
2. My dad is _____ at me for crashing his car last week.
3. Let's _____. I'm getting so tired.
4. Hey _____, what are we doing this weekend?
5. Let's hang out at my _____ tonight.
6. I'm so _____ that I didn't get into UBC.
7. My dad is super _____ but also quite entertaining.
8. Just _____ it for 3 minutes.
9. That amusement park? It's _____. Don't waste your time going.

Answers

1. high hopes
2. pissed
3. split
4. ya'll
5. pad
6. bummed
7. corny
8. nuke
9. rinky-dink

Junkies

Ted and Sam are in a bad part of town.

Ted: Hey, can we stop and **grab** a coffee? I'm **running out of gas** here.

Sam: Can you **hold out** for a few minutes? There are so many **junkies** and **cops** around this part of town. I try to never stop here if I can avoid it. It's just too **dicey**.

Ted: **Totes**. I can **hold out** for a bit.

Sam: Sorry.

Ted: **No sweat**. Hey, what about going to Bean Around the World on the Drive? That place really **hits the spot**.

Sam: Awesome. Thanks for understanding.

Vocabulary

Grab: Get; pick up.

Running out of gas: Getting tired.

Totes: Totally; of course.

Hold out: Wait.

Junkies: People addicted to drugs.

Cops: Police officers.

Dicey: Sketchy; not safe.

No sweat: No problem.

Hits the spot: Describes something that's satisfying.

Practice

Fill in the blanks with the correct word or phrase

1. I know Taco Casa is so unhealthy but that really _____.
2. Can you _____ a pizza on your way home for dinner?
3. Let's _____ for a better offer.
4. Call the _____. I think a robbery is happening across the street.
5. Oh, _____. That wasn't a big deal to me at all.
6. Can we call it a day? I'm _____.
7. There are so many _____ in downtown Vancouver.
8. Let's hit the gym before work tomorrow. _____.
9. I think this ski run is kind of _____. Let's take the easier one.

Answers

1. hit the spot
2. grab
3. hold out
4. cops
5. no sweat
6. running of gas
7. junkies
8. totes
9. dicey

Karen

Eddy and Cindy are talking about their aunt Anne.

Eddy: How was the family dinner?

Cindy: It **sucked**, **big time**.

Eddy: What happened?

Cindy: Oh you know Anne. She's basically a **Karen** every time she leaves the house. She was yelling at the waitress about nothing. And then refused to pay for her dinner.

Eddy: **I can't even**.

Cindy: It gets worse. She hit the **booze** and got **blackout drunk**. We had to drive her home afterwards. And then my mom made me **Uber** there in the morning to get her car for her.

Eddy: Not **cool**. I hate stuff like that.

Vocabulary

Sucked: Describes something terrible.

Big time: In a large way.

Karen: Generally refers to an obnoxious, entitled, middle-aged white lady.

I can't even: Describes an event that is too frustrating or annoying to even talk about.

Booze: Alcohol.

Blackout drunk: Drinking alcohol to the point where you can't remember what happened.

Uber: A ride-sharing service. It can be used as a noun or a verb.

Cool: Hip; awesome; great.

Practice

Fill in the blanks with the correct word or phrase.

1. Hey, it's so _____ that you got a better job.
2. _____. I can't believe he said that.
3. It _____ when I lost my job but I found a better one quickly.
4. Why don't we _____ home after the concert?
5. I'm getting old. I can't remember the last time I got _____.
6. Stop being a _____! It's embarrassing.
7. Let's pick up some _____ after we go to the grocery store.
8. I want a smoke _____ but my husband will kill me.

Answers

1. cool
2. I can't even
3. sucked
4. Uber
5. blackout drunk
6. Karen
7. booze
8. big time

No Biggie

Keith is asking his girlfriend Mandy for some help.

Keith: Hey **babe**, can you help me out with the garden this weekend?

Mandy: **You bet**.

Keith: You're so **chill**. That's why I love you. Plus, you're **hot** too.

Mandy: You really know how to flatter a girl. It's **no biggie**.

Keith: Okay, let's **crack open a bottle** when we're done and **kick back** a bit.

Mandy: **Wicked**.

Vocabulary

Babe: Honey, sweetie (said to someone you're in a romantic relationship with).

You bet: Agreeing to something.

Chill: Describes someone who is generally relaxed about things.

Hot: Describes someone good-looking.

No biggie: Not a big deal.

Crack open a bottle: Open a bottle of wine.

Kick back: Relax.

Wicked: Awesome; great.

Practice

Fill in the blanks with the correct word or phrase

1. That's so _____ about your new job!

2. Will you give me a ride to the airport on Tuesday? _____.

3. Oh, _____. I don't mind at all.

4. Hey _____, let's get sushi tonight.

5. Your new boyfriend is so _____.

6. Let's _____ and BBQ tonight.

7. When should we _____? Is it too early?

Answers

1. wicked

2. you bet

3. no biggie

4. babe

5. hot

6. kick back/chill

7. crack open a bottle

Cancelled

Tim and Sara are talking about their high-school classmate, Sam.

Sara: Hey dude, did you hear that Sam got **cancelled**?

Tim: No, what **went down**?

Sara: Well, he **straight up** said a bunch of homophobic things to Lucy in front of so many people. People even recorded it with their phones.

Tim: Why am I so **out of the loop**? Anyway, What a **loser**. Who does that?

Sara: Yeah, super **sketchy**. He has a such **a big mouth**.

Tim: I hope Principal Brown **brings the hammer down**.

Sara: Nah, she's probably going to do nothing, like usual.

Vocabulary

Cancelled: Describes someone who is rejected or dismissed because of their bad behaviour.

Went down: Happened.

Straight up: Honestly.

Out of the loop: Not knowing some information.

Loser: Describes someone who is not cool.

Sketchy: Describes someone who can't be trusted.

A big mouth: Describes someone who talks too much.

Brings the hammer down: Punishes.

Practice

Fill in the blanks with the correct word or phrase

1. She always _____. Watch out.
2. That hockey player got _____ because of his racist comments.
3. I'm so _____ when it comes to office politics but I like it that way.
4. Does anyone else find that new guy super _____?
5. I _____ want to tell her to just sit down and be quiet.
6. My uncle Tony has such _____. I hate inviting him to family gatherings.
7. What _____ between you two?
8. My last boyfriend was such a _____. Breaking up with him was the best decision I've ever made.

Answers

1. brings the hammer down
2. cancelled
3. out of the loop
4. sketchy
5. straight up
6. a big mouth
7. went down
8. loser

Peanuts

Lucy and Annie are talking about their jobs.

Lucy: Hey, what's up?

Annie: Oh, you know. Just working for **peanuts** as a **paper-pusher** at NewTech.

Lucy: Sorry to hear that. Are you **hard up** for cash?

Annie: A little but I'm **getting by**. Why?

Lucy: I know a way to make **a quick buck** but you'll have to work Friday and Saturday nights.

Annie: Nah, I'm already **maxed out** with my night courses too. Remember when we used to **goof off** and smoke **joints** during lunch in high school?

Lucy: Those were the days. Now we have these ridiculous **white collar** jobs.

Vocabulary

Peanuts: A small amount of money.

Paper-pusher: Someone who does admin at work but doesn't make any real decisions.

Hard up: Describes someone who doesn't have any money.

Getting by: Describes someone who can pay the bills but doesn't have a lot of extra money.

A quick buck: Easy money.

Maxed out: At capacity.

Goof off: Have fun by ignoring some responsibilities.

Joints: Marijuana in cigarette form.

White collar: Describes a job that doesn't require manual labour; a desk or office job.

Practice

Fill in the blanks with the correct word or phrase

1. I need to find a _____ job. My body can't handle construction anymore.
2. He's just a _____. The real decisions get made by Cindy.
3. I'm _____ but I'm nervous about how expensive having kids will be.
4. We're _____. Sorry, we can't squeeze you in.
5. Bring some _____ to the beach, okay?
6. If you want to make _____, check out my company. They're hiring temporary workers.
7. Ted loves to _____ at school and his grades are suffering because of it.
8. I'm so tired of working for _____. There has to be a better option.
9. If you're _____, why not move back in with your parents?

Answers

1. white collar
2. paper-pusher
3. getting by
4. maxed out
5. joints
6. a quick buck
7. goof off
8. peanuts
9. hard up

No Big Deal

Anne and Jen are talking about Jen's old job.

Anne: Hey Jen, how's your job going these days?

Jen: Oh, you didn't hear? It was **a bust**.

Anne: Oh no! That's terrible. What happened?

Jen: **No big deal**. I got a new job the next week. Anyway, the **head honcho** was so **chintzy** and kept trying to **rip me off** on my paycheck.

Anne: Anything to make a **buck**, right? That's so bad.

Jen: **YOLO**. I'm so happy I quit. My new job is so much better.

Vocabulary

Bust: Describes something that didn't work out.

No big deal: It's not a large problem.

Head honcho: The boss.

Chintzy: Very cheap.

Rip me off: Steal money from.

Buck: Dollar.

YOLO: You only live once!

Practice

Fill in the blanks with the correct word or phrase.

1. Go for it. _____!
2. My uncle is _____ but he's also a millionaire because of it.
3. Do you have a _____ to spare?
4. Oh, _____. I don't care about stuff like that.
5. The _____ wants to meet with me next week.
6. Did that guy just try to _____? Did you see that?
7. That program turned out to be a _____.

Answers

1. YOLO
2. chintzy
3. buck
4. no big deal
5. head honcho
6. rip me off
7. bust

Chow Down

Gary and Andy are talking about their teenage kids.

Gary: How are the kids these days?

Andy: Oh you know, they basically **scarf down** all the food in the house at every possible moment. And then **zone out** playing video games for hours.

Gary: Same here. My kids **chow down** on all the good stuff after I go grocery shopping and it's gone in a day.

Andy: Mine **go nuts** for pizza. Whenever I get take-out, I have to say, "**Hold your horses!** Leave a piece for me."

Gary: You sound almost **laid back**. My kids go **psycho** for it too. I got smart and now take some out for my wife and I before I even bring it into the house.

Andy: You're **winning at life** my friend.

Vocabulary

Scarf down: Eat a lot very quickly.

Zone out: Relax; lose concentration or focus.

Chow down: Eat food.

Go nuts: Go crazy for something because you love it.

Hold your horses: Wait.

Laid back: Describes someone who is relaxed about something.

Go psycho: Act irrationally or crazy.

Winning at life: You have life figured out; good move!

Practice

Fill in the blanks with the correct word or phrase

1. You know you're _____ when the kids clean up their dishes without you asking them!
2. Is it time to _____? I'm hungry.
3. My kids _____ ice cream like it's water.
4. _____. You'll have to wait in line like the rest of us.
5. I'm scared he's going to _____ if I confront him about this. Will you come with me?
6. I always _____ in math class; it's so boring.
7. Let's _____ and finish this by 5:00.
8. I want to be more _____ but I always have a million things going on in my head.

Answers

1. winning at life
2. chow down
3. scarf down
4. hold your horses
5. go psycho
6. zone out
7. go nuts
8. laid back

Party Animal

Kevin and Mark are talking about the party they were at last night.

Kevin: Dude, you're such a **party animal**! You were so **wasted** last night. It was **epic**.

Mark: Yeah, I had **a blast** until I ran into my **ex**.

Kevin: Seriously? I didn't know that. That was why you left so early?

Mark: Yeah, she's **cray** and I didn't want to deal with her. She **ghosted** me after dating for six months. Who does that?

Kevin: She's **basic**. You're better off without her.

Mark: Yeah, I know. But I'm still angry so I didn't want to have a big **showdown** after I'd been drinking so much.

Kevin: You're a wise man, my friend.

Vocabulary

Party animal: Someone who likes to go to parties and drink a lot.

Wasted: Drunk.

Epic: Describes something that happened which is amazing or awesome.

A blast: A lot of fun.

Cray: Crazy

Ghosted: Suddenly stopped responding to messages without explanation, usually in a dating relationship.

Basic: Describes someone who is boring, without originality or style.

Showdown: Big fight.

Practice

Fill in the blanks with the correct word or phrase.

1. I think you two will need to have a _____ eventually.
2. That guy is such a _____. I've never seen him without a drink in his hand.
3. My boss is _____. I can't believe he expects me to work for free on weekends.
4. That girl is so _____. Why does everyone like her so much?
5. I had _____ camping this year.
6. That guy I was talking to online just _____ me.
7. Dude! Your jump was _____.
8. Let's get _____ this weekend.

Answers

1. showdown
2. party animal
3. cray
4. basic
5. a blast
6. ghosted
7. epic
8. wasted

Speak of the Devil

Jerry and Linda are talking about Kenny's new look.

Jerry: Have you seen Kenny lately? He **looks like a million bucks,** always wearing **flashy** clothes and driving his fancy new car.

Linda: I haven't seen him lately but guys like that are **a dime a dozen in this town.** They all made their money in finance, I think.

Jerry: Speak of the devil! I think I see him coming in the door right now! Let's call him over.

Linda: I don't want to **beat around the bush** so I'll just say it. I don't like Kenny! He **ripped me off** on his old TV that he sold me. It was hanging on by its' **last legs**.

Jerry: Let's **get out of here** then before he sees us.

Vocabulary

Speak of the devil: The person you are talking about appears at that exact moment. For example, you are talking about a coworker and then they walk into the room right then.

Looks like a million bucks: To look attractive or well put together.

A dime a dozen: Something that is very common, not special.

Beat around the bush: Avoid talking about something important, or not getting to the main point directly.

Ripped me off: To make a bad deal with someone. To be stolen from.

Get out of here: To leave a place, usually quickly.

Flashy: Bright, shiny, expensive.

Last legs: Something that is close to breaking/stopping/not working.

Practice

Fill in the blanks with the correct word or phrase.

1. Tim _____ these days with his new haircut.

2. Job offers like that are _____.

3. I want to _____ so badly! I hate this school.

4. "Oh, _____! We were just talking about you!"

5. Honestly, I hate that my boss loves to _____. I wish he'd just get to the point.

6. I'm so embarrassed that he_____.

7. My brother got a _____ new haircut in preparation for his job interview.

8. I'm going to have to buy a new car. This one is on its' _____.

Answers

1. looks like a million bucks

2. a dime a dozen

3. get out of here

4. speak of the devil

5. beat around the bush

6. ripped me off

7. flashy

8. last legs

Plus One

Ed is inviting Cindy to be his date for a wedding.

Ed: Hey, did you hear that Tom and Sara are **tying the knot** next month? Do you want to be my **plus one**?

Cindy: Is there an **open bar**?

Ed: They have **deep pockets**. I'm sure there will be.

Cindy: Okay. I'm **up for it** then. We can **pig out** on wedding **grub**, get **drunk** and cut up the dance floor!

Ed: I have the exact same vision. I'm **pumped**. I'll send you all the details but it's on May 23 at 4:00.

Cindy: **Rad**! Thanks for inviting me.

Vocabulary

Tying the knot: Getting married.

Plus one: A date for a party, wedding, or other event.

Open bar: As much free alcohol as you want at a wedding or party.

Deep pockets: Describes someone who has lots of money.

Up for it: I'll do it; I'm game; I'll go.

Pig out: Eat a lot.

Grub: Food.

Drunk: Describes someone who has had too much alcohol.

Pumped: Excited.

Rad: Awesome; great.

Practice

Fill in the blanks with the correct word or phrase.

1. That's so _____ about your new job!

2. Who's _____? I haven't heard the latest gossip.

3. Wherever you want to go for lunch, I'm _____.

4. I hope there's an _____ at our Christmas party.

5. Let's get some _____. I'm famished.

6. I'm so _____ to see Tony. It's been years.

7. My company has _____ and money is no object.

8. Do you want to be my _____ for my cousin's wedding?

9. I want to _____ tonight! I skipped lunch. How about ABC buffet?

10. I can't get _____ tonight—I have to work early tomorrow.

Answers

1. rad

2. tying the knot

3. up for it

4. open bar

5. grub

6. pumped

7. deep pockets

8. plus one

9. pig out

10. drunk

Hit the Sack

Jerry and Larry are talking about being very busy.

Jerry: I have to **hit the sack.** I'm so tired right now.

Larry: Have you been **burning the midnight oil** lately?

Jerry: Yeah, I've been trying to study for this test. I should have started earlier.

Larry: Well, **better late than never**. But, make sure to get enough sleep. If you're tired, you won't remember anything.

Jerry: You're right. It was **many moons** ago that I got a decent night's sleep.

Larry: Don't give up. I think you'll **ace** it.

Jerry: Well, here's hoping I **come up trumps**! Time to **knuckle down** and get to work.

Vocabulary

Hit the sack: Go to bed.

Many moons: A long time ago.

Burning the midnight oil: Staying up late working or studying.

Better late than never: Encouragement after getting a late start to something.

Ace: To get a high mark on a test or do well at something like a job interview.

Come up trumps: To get exactly what is needed at the last minute.

Knuckle down: To focus deeply on something.

Practice

Fill in the blanks with the correct word or phrase.

1. Don't forget to _____ early. It's your big game tomorrow!

2. Although it was _____ ago, I still think about my ex-boyfriend.

3. I've been _____ lately, working a second job.

4. Honestly, it's _____ but he dropped the ball on this project.

5. You won't _____ the test unless you study.

6. That guy has an uncanny ability to always _____.

7. It's the last thing I want to do but I know it's time to _____ and study.

Answers

1. hit the sack

2. many moons

3. burning the midnight oil

4. better late than never

5. ace

6. come up trumps

7. knuckle down

Ballin'

Sam is talking to Edward about his new car.

Sam: Dude! Your car is **ballin'**. You **killed it** with that color and those rims.

Edward: Yeah, it's **the bomb** for sure. What are you driving these days?

Sam: Basically **a lemon**. I'm hoping to get a new one when I get my bonus. Do you get lots of **chicks** with that thing?

Edward: Oh, you know me. I have a cool car but I'm hopelessly **out of style**! Hahaha.

Sam: Nah bro, put some **shades** on and we'll go **cruising**. You'll do **alright**.

Edward: Yeah! That sounds great.

Vocabulary

Ballin': Describes something cool or fashionable.

Killed it: Did really well at something.

The bomb: Something amazing or awesome.

A lemon: A car that is always breaking down.

Chicks: Young women who are attractive.

Out of style: Describes someone who isn't fashionable.

Shades: Sunglasses.

Cruising: Driving around, trying to meet people.

Alright: Good.

Practice

Fill in the blanks with the correct word or phrase

1. Hey, you'll do _____ on this test. Don't worry.
2. I'm so _____ and I don't even care.
3. That teacher is _____.
4. Let's go _____ tonight. I'm bored.
5. Where are all the _____ at?
6. You _____ on that presentation!
7. I need to grab my _____ before we go.
8. He's _____ with that fancy new car of his.
9. Your car is _____. It's time to stop throwing money away fixing it and just get a new one.

Answers

1. alright
2. out of style
3. the bomb
4. cruising
5. chicks
6. killed it
7. shades
8. ballin'
9. a lemon

From Dawn Till Dusk

Eric and Mandy are talking about working a lot.

Eric: How's work going **these days**?

Mandy: The usual. I have to work **from dawn till dusk**. We have all these **strict deadlines** from clients and are always **running out of time**.

Eric: Can you **cut back on** your hours? That's terrible not having any **free time**.

Mandy: Not if I want to **get ahead** in this industry. I'd love to **take my time** on projects. But, that's **not going to cut it**.

Vocabulary

These days: Lately.

From dawn till dusk: Working very long hours (early morning to late at night).

Strict deadlines: A definite time when something needs to be finished.

Running out of time: Lacking time to finish or do something.

Cut back on: Reduce.

Free time: Leisure time when not working or studying.

Get ahead: Make gains, especially compared to other people.

Take my time: Not hurry.

Not going to cut it: Something you do isn't good enough.

Practice

Fill in the blank with the correct word or phrase.

1. Please do it again. That's _____.
2. I hate having to work under _____. It's very stressful.
3. In my _____, I love to hang out with friends.
4. I have to work _____ during the year-end.
5. I'd love to _____ my drinking but it's difficult around the holidays.
6. I'd love to _____ and make a good decision about which program to take.
7. It's difficult to _____ in Vancouver when housing is so expensive.
8. _____, I'm trying to get in better shape.
9. We're _____ and will need to stay late tonight.

Answers

1. not going to cut it
2. strict deadlines
3. free time
4. from dawn till dusk
5. cut back on
6. take my time
7. get ahead
8. these days
9. running out of time

Swag

Angela and Lucy are talking about a gig tonight.

Angela: Hey, did I hear that you're playing a **gig** tonight at the Metro?

Lucy: Yeah, do you want to come?

Angela: Are you giving away any **swag**?

Lucy: No **freebies**! It's such a myth that musicians make **megabucks**. Most of us are **struggling to make ends meet**.

Angela: Okay, okay! I'll come anyways. What time?

Lucy: 10:45.

Angela: So late. But I'll **catch some Z's** now so I'll be good for later. **Break a leg**!

Vocabulary

Gig: A concert or performance, somewhat informal.

Swag: Something free you get at an event.

Freebies: Something free, in any situation.

Megabucks: Lots of money.

Struggling to make ends meet: Finding it difficult to make enough money to pay all the bills.

Catch some Z's: Get some sleep.

Break a leg: An expression to say, "Good luck" to someone just about to go on stage.

Practice

Fill in the blanks with the correct word or phrase.

1. Hey, _____ tonight, okay?

2. They don't pay her the _____ for nothing!

3. Did you get some good _____ at the conference?

4. _____ and we'll talk later.

5. Let's go to Costco on Saturday afternoon. They always have so many _____.

6. Can you come to my _____ this weekend?

7. Sid is _____. Should we try to help him out?

Answers

1. break a leg

2. megabucks

3. swag

4. catch some Z's

5. freebies

6. gig

7. struggling to make ends meet

Stuck in a Traffic Jam

Richard is stuck in a traffic jam and telling Linda that he'll be late for their appointment.

Richard: Linda? Hi. Sorry, I'm going to be late for our **coffee date**. There's a **traffic jam** somewhere up ahead. We're crawling along at a **snail's pace**.

Linda: Oh no. What time will you be here?

Richard: It's **impossible to predict**. There's a lot of traffic. I'll be as fast as I can.

Linda: Okay. Keep me updated, please. I need to leave in about an hour to pick up my kids from school.

Richard: I didn't know you needed to leave at a specific time. I'll **keep you updated.**

Linda: Sure. **Better late than never**! I was **in the same boat** yesterday meeting my husband.

Vocabulary

Coffee date: Meeting with someone over coffee. May, or may not be a romantic date.

Traffic jam: Cars that aren't moving quickly because of an accident or heavy traffic up ahead.

Snail's pace: Very slow.

Impossible to predict: Unable to give an exact time, answer, etc.

Keep you updated: Give me information as you know it.

Better late than never: It's better to do something not on time than not at all.

In the same boat: Experiencing the same thing.

Practice

Fill in the blanks with the correct word or phrase.

1. There's a big _____ up ahead. Let's take another route.

2. It was due 3 weeks ago but _____.

3. I hope Toronto will win the Stanley Cup but it's _____.

4. Everything in this company moves at a _____.

5. Are you free for a _____ next Tuesday morning?

6. You and Tom are _____.

7. I'll _____ every week.

Answers

1. traffic jam

2. better late than never

3. impossible to predict

4. snail's pace

5. coffee date

6. in the same boat

7. keep you updated

Down to Earth

Casey is talking to Dan about his crush on Tina.

Dan: Hey, so what's up with you and Tina?

Casey: Seriously, nothing. I have **a crush** on her but I'm too nervous to ask her out. Every time I talk to her, I can never bring myself to do it.

Dan: Stop being such a **chicken**. She's **down to Earth**. She won't be mean if the answer is no.

Casey: I'm just scared of rejection I guess.

Dan: Well, **it's not rocket science**! Just talk to her and see what the **vibe** is. I'm **rooting for you**.

Casey: Give it **another shot**! I'll buy you lunch if you do, no matter what the answer is!

Vocabulary

Crush: Initial liking of someone in a romantic way.

Chicken: Describes someone who is scared of something.

Down to Earth: Easy-going.

It's not rocket science: It's not that difficult to do.

Vibe: Feeling.

Rooting for you: Cheering for you.

Another shot: One more try.

Practice

Fill in the blanks with the correct word or phrase.

1. Just give it _____. I'm sure you'll get it.

2. Don't be such a _____ and just do it!

3. Honestly, _____. I have no idea what's taking him so long.

4. We're all _____.

5. She's very _____ and easy to talk to.

6. Did you hear that Ted has a _____ on Sally?

7. What's the _____ like?

Answers

1. another shot

2. chicken

3. it's not rocket science

4. rooting for you

5. down to Earth

6. crush

7. vibe

Sit Tight

Jason and Linda are talking about when to leave to get the train.

Jason: Hey, let's get moving! **Time is money.**

Linda: Sit tight. I need to grab a few things before we go.

Jason: Come on. We have to get to the train station on time. I hate always being the **bad guy** about stuff like this.

Linda: Well, to be fair, you've been as **clear as mud** about what time we needed to leave. Traffic won't be as bad as you think.

Jason: There are always **traffic jams** at this time. Let's **get a move on.**

Linda: Okay, I'll be ready **in the blink of an eye**. Stop bugging me!

Vocabulary

Sit tight: Wait patiently and don't take any action right now.

Clear as mud: Confusing or not easy to understand.

Time is money: To try to get someone to work faster or more efficiently.

Traffic jams: When cars aren't moving quickly because it's busy.

Get a move on: Hurry up.

Bad guy: Someone who always has bad news/enforces a rule.

In the blink of an eye: In a short amount of time.

Practice

Fill in the blanks with the correct word or phrase.

1. If you leave after 8 am, there will be lots of _____.
2. Let's _____. I don't want to be late for school.
3. I try to always remember that _____.
4. I had a terrible teacher in high school. His explanations were as _____.
5. _____ while I check and see what time the movie starts.
6. I hate to be the _____ but you need to get it together or you're going to get fired.
7. Don't miss the eclipse. It'll happen _____.

Answers

1. traffic jams
2. get a move on
3. time is money
4. clear as mud
5. Sit tight
6. bad guy
7. in the blink of an eye

Have a Blast

Sandy is trying to convince Danielle to come out to a club that night.

Sandy: Hey, I heard you weren't coming tonight? You know we'll **have a blast**.

Danielle: Nah, that music at that club is so **vanilla**.

Sandy: **I feel you** but I also think you should **lighten up** a bit! The music doesn't matter as much as a hang with all your **peeps.**

Danielle: I still think I'll **take a rain check**.

Sandy: Lets be real. The **FOMO** is going to get you so I'll see you there.

Danielle: If you do, you do. If you don't, you don't.

Sandy: Okay fine.

Vocabulary

Have a blast: Have fun.

Vanilla: Boring; not interesting.

I feel you: I understand.

Lighten up: Relax; chill out.

Peeps: Friends.

Take a rain check: Do the activity or event some other time.

FOMO: Fear of missing out.

Practice

Fill in the blanks with the correct word or phrase.

1. I don't care what you say. _____ is a real thing.

2. I think you'll get along better with Tony if you _____.

3. He's a nice guy but very _____.

4. Can I _____? I have a headache.

5. _____ but I still don't think it's the right decision.

6. Where are all my _____ at?

7. You'll _____ tonight! Just enjoy it.

Answers

1. FOMO

2. lighten up

3. vanilla

4. take a rain check

5. I feel you

6. peeps

7. have a blast

When Pigs Fly

Jerry and Linda are talking about their kids.

Jerry: My kids are **buttering me up** because they don't want to have to help put up **Christmas lights.**

Linda: You're lucky that you can get some help **once in a while**. My kids never **pitch in** for stuff like that. **When pigs fly**, right?

Jerry: Ah, it's all **smoke and mirrors** at my house usually. My kids **make a show out of** cleaning up after themselves after dinner but their rooms are still like a **pigsty**.

Linda: What have we gotten ourselves into?

Vocabulary

When pigs fly: Something that is very unlikely to happen.

Pitch in: To contribute to or help with something.

Buttering me up: To flatter or please someone because you want something in return. For example, a child who is extra nice to their parents around Christmas because they want an expensive video game system.

Smoke and mirrors: Flashy things that distract from what is real.

Christmas lights: Lights on houses for decoration around Christmas.

Once in a while: Sometimes.

Make a show out of: To do something in a flashy way.

Pigsty: Usually refers to a very messy room or space.

Practice

Fill in the blanks with the correct word or phrase.

1. I like to let loose _____.

2. His presentation was all _____. No real substance.

3. My kids love to help me put up _____.

4. We all _____ every Saturday morning to clean up the house.

5. My kid's bedroom is a _____.

6. My mom always used to say, "_____" when I asked her for money!

7. I know when my kids are _____ but I fall for it anyway. Their sweet smiles!

8. I hate that my coworkers always _____ finishing even the smallest task.

Answers

1. once in a while

2. smoke and mirrors

3. Christmas lights

4. pitch in

5. pigsty

6. When pigs fly

7. buttering me up

8. make a show out of

Running Late

Zeke wants to let Sid know that he is running late.

Zeke: Sid. Hi. So sorry but I'm **running late** and can't meet you for dinner at 6:30.

Sid: Oh, okay. You're late **once in a blue moon**! I don't mind. What time do you think you'll get here?

Zeke: By 7:00 at the latest, I think. There was a **car crash** ahead of me on the highway.

Sid: Oh no! Is it cleared?

Zeke: It will be soon. It looks like the police are finishing up now and traffic is moving slowly. Hopefully, we'll be **rolling soon**.

Sid: Sure. See you when you get here. **No rush**. I'll just have a glass of wine to **kill time**. It isn't terrible, to say the least.

Zeke: Can't complain about that, right? Thanks for understanding. I appreciate it. Oh, and it's my treat so **order a bottle**, okay?

Vocabulary

Running late: Being behind schedule.

Once in a blue moon: Not often.

Car crash: Accident.

Rolling soon: Will start moving shortly.

No rush: Don't hurry.

Kill time: Do something to fill time.

Order a bottle: Get a bottle of wine, instead of just a glass at a restaurant.

Practice

Fill in the blanks with the correct word or phrase.

1. Hey Ted, I'm sorry but I'm _____.

2. I'd love to see the report but it's _____. I can wait.

3. I only smoke _____.

4. There's a _____ on Whyte Ave. Let's find a different route.

5. I usually watch Netflix when I have to _____.

6. Let's _____ for the whole table.

7. Get ready! We'll be _____ on all these new contracts.

Answers

1. running late

2. no rush

3. once in a blue moon

4. car crash

5. kill time

6. order a bottle

7. rolling soon

Feeling Under the Weather

Jerry and Linda are talking about not feeling well.

Linda: Hey, what's up with you these days?

Jerry: I've been sick for months now. I'm started to get worried about it.

Linda: I know you're **feeling under the weather** but **this too shall pass.**

Jerry: Thanks Linda, I appreciate you **checking in on** me every day.

Linda: It's the least I can do. You've helped me with so many things over the years. Just don't **kick the bucket** on me, okay?

Vocabulary

Feeling under the weather: Not feeling well; feeling sick.

Couch potato: Someone who spends lots of time on the couch watching TV or movies or playing video games. Not active.

An apple a day keeps the doctor away: Eating healthy keeps you from getting sick.

This too shall pass: A bad time period that will eventually end.

Checking in on: To see how someone is doing.

It's the least I can do: No problem; it's a small thing, usually when you feel like you should do more.

Kick the bucket: Die.

Practice

Fill in the blanks with the correct word or phrase.

1. My dad keeps phoning and _____ me. It's almost too much!

2. I keep nagging my son to get active because he's such a _____.

3. I called in sick because I was feeling a bit _____.

4. I'm convinced that the saying, "_____" does work!

5. My son has been pretty down lately but I told him that, "_____."

6. Lunch is on me. _____, seeing as you've been making me meals all week.

7. I hope that I don't _____ before I'm 80 but I'm nervous about how much I smoke!

Answers

1. checking in on

2. couch potato

3. under the weather

4. An apple a day keeps the doctor away

5. This too shall pass

6. It's the least I can do

7. kick the bucket

Before You Go

If you found this book useful, please leave a review wherever you bought it. It will help other English learners, like yourself find this resource.

You may also want to check out this book: Advanced English Conversation Dialogues by Jackie Bolen. You can find it wherever you like to buy books. Improve your English vocabulary in a fun and interesting way.

Made in the USA
Monee, IL
26 February 2023

28748753R00035